the Weekend Crafter®

Knitting

the
Weekend
Crafter®

Knitting

20 Simple & Stylish Wearables
for Beginners

CATHERINE HAM

LARK
BOOKS

A Division of Sterling Publishing Co., Inc.
New York

For Ron

EDITOR:
PAIGE GILCHRIST

ART DIRECTOR & PRODUCTION:
CELIA NARANJO

SYTLIST:
TOM METCALF

COVER DESIGNER:
BARBARA ZARETSKY

PHOTOGRAPHY:
EVAN BRACKEN

ILLUSTRATIONS:
ORRIN LUNDGREN

ASSISTANT EDITORS:
VERONIKA ALICE GUNTER
RAIN NEWCOMB

ART ASSISTANT:
SHANNON YOKELEY

ART INTERN:
LORELEI BUCKLEY

EDITORIAL ASSISTANCE:
DELORES GOSNELL

Library of Congress Cataloging-in-Publication Data

Ham, Catherine.
  Knitting: 20 simple & stylish wearables for beginners / Catherine Ham.
    p. cm. -- (Weekend crafter)
   ISBN 1-57990-351-7 (paper)
   1. Knitting--Patterns. 2. Knit goods. I. Title: Knitting twenty simple and stylish wearables for beginners. II. Title. III. Series.

  TT825. H355 2002
  746.43'20432--dc21

                                          2002028789

10 9 8 7 6 5 4 3 2 1

First Edition

Published by Lark Books, a division of
Sterling Publishing Co., Inc.
387 Park Avenue South, New York, N.Y. 10016

© 2003, Catherine Ham

Distributed in Canada by Sterling Publishing,
c/o Canadian Manda Group, One Atlantic Ave., Suite 105
Toronto, Ontario, Canada M6K 3E7

Distributed in the U.K. by Guild of Master Craftsman Publications Ltd., Castle Place,
166 High Street, Lewes, East Sussex, England
BN7 1XU
Tel: (+ 44) 1273 477374, Fax: (+ 44) 1273 478606,
Email: pubs@thegmcgroup.com, Web: www.gmcpublications.com

Distributed in Australia by Capricorn Link (Australia) Pty Ltd.,
P.O. Box 704, Windsor, NSW 2756 Australia

If you have questions or comments about this book, please contact:
Lark Books
67 Broadway
Asheville, NC 28801
(828) 253-0467
Printed in China

1-57990-351-7

CONTENTS

INTRODUCTION

KNIT SOMETHING simple and rewarding with the help of this book, whether you're a very new knitter or a more experienced knitter looking for a fast, fun project. These patterns offer a great way to try out a new design or technique, and they'll showcase your knitting skills. Many of them also make excellent use of your yarn odds and ends.

Consider this book your own personal "recipe book" of basic designs you can use again and again. Don't limit yourself to the designs as I've spelled them out. You could apply the color work on the kid's sweater to all manner of projects—it would make a wonderfully textured pillow, for example. The very simple lacy pattern on the Crop Top, page 66, can be used on a different sweater or on the sleeve of an otherwise plain sweater. Make margin notes, fill the book with little sticky page markers, and refine and tweak the patterns to suit yourself.

You can also use several of this book's ideas to build up a stash to dip into for that unexpected gift you always seem to need at the last minute, or to give yourself a head start on your holiday gift making. Many of the designs are ideal for quick and easy giving. GoogliBug (see page 36) makes a whimsical present for just about anyone, hats and scarves are always welcome, and who doesn't need a gift for a baby every now and then? Keep a handsome basket nearby filled with a copy of your pattern, suitable yarns, and buttons. You'll be amazed how much you can get done at odd moments to add to your gift supply.

To prepare for a lovely knitting weekend, try to take care of chores and errands ahead of time, so you have as few interruptions as possible, then let the answering machine do its job. Set up a comfortable knitting spot, if you're able to spend most of this wonderful knitting time at home, and organize yourself with everything you need to work at your most relaxed.

First and most obvious, do you have yarn? Ideally, you'll want to get familiar with the yarn you intend to use. If you haven't used it before, make a gauge swatch (I tell you how on page 11), so you know how it knits up and won't have any surprises. Once you're satisfied with your gauge swatch, put a tag or label on it indicating the needle size you found most suitable to achieve the correct gauge. It's a good idea to get this out of the way before your knitting weekend begins.

If your yarn comes in hanks, wind it into balls ahead of time (check page 10). Do you have all the tools you need? If not, now is the time to gather together a set of the essentials (see my list, page 8). Read through the pattern to be sure you understand what you'll be doing and that you have all the necessary materials.

OK, so you're all set up, but perhaps you won't be sitting at home during this gorgeous knitting weekend. Could be, you'll be watching proudly from the sidelines at a sporting event, or working away on a long car ride. If so, pack everything you need into your knitting tote. It's a good idea to make a copy or even multiple copies of the pattern you'll be using, so you don't have to cart the book around with you. Include a pen or pencil, so you can easily make notes on the copy. You may need to pack your favorite techniques book, too, or a photocopy of the relevant pages, if you'll need a reference.

The projects that follow are designed to be quick and simple. They can generally be completed in an average weekend. Of course, that will depend on your personal pace and on what exactly an average weekend means for you. Keep in mind it's not written in stone that you must finish by Sunday evening at all costs. What is important is that you enjoy what you're doing while adding to your knitting know-how and expertise.

KNITTING BASICS

IN THIS SECTION, I will briefly remind you of the fundamentals required to knit the projects that follow. It's important that you also have a copy of a good how-to-knit book to which you can refer.

TOOLS & SUPPLIES

Needles

An amazing variety of knitting needles is available, and it won't be long before you've built up a large collection of them. Needles come in two basic types—circular and straight—and in a variety of materials, from metal and plastic to bamboo and rosewood. When buying needles for yourself, remember that there is no single, correct needle type or material. These are personal choices, and you'll find yourself tending to use one type more than another. Just use what feels most comfortable to you.

Other Tools

- small pair of scissors or snips
- tapestry needles for sewing up seams (these have large eyes and blunt tips)
- tape measure
- stitch holders and safety pins
- needle gauge

Add a notebook and pen, and you have the most essential tools you should keep in your knitting bag. As for the perfect knitting bag…well, that's a subject for a whole other book!

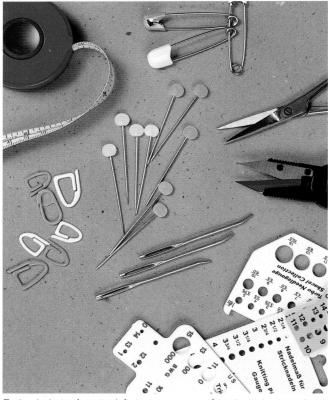

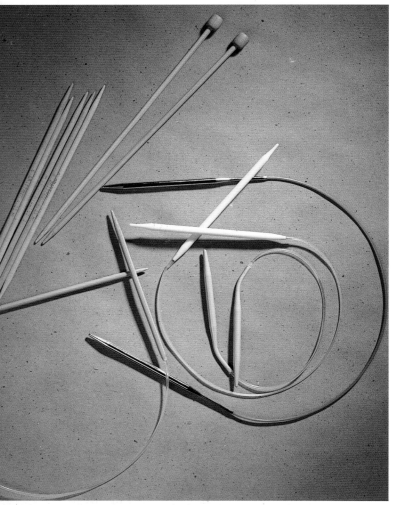

A selection of knitting needles

Tools, clockwise from top left: tape measure, safety pins, scissors, snips, needle gauges, tapestry needles, straight pins, stitch holders

Then, of Course, There's the Yarn

Yarns are made from animal fibers or plant fibers or they're man-made (i.e., chemically manufactured). Animal fibers include wool, mohair, alpaca, and angora, while plant fibers include cotton and linen. Natural fibers are often combined with synthetic yarns to create yarns with special characteristics. An acrylic/wool mixture, for example, will have some of the properties of a wool fiber, together with the easy-care qualities of a synthetic.

Yarns are spun in various ways to achieve a particular effect, which gives the knitted fabric a distinctive look. For example, yarn may be very smooth or have loops or nubs twisted with it, resulting in a highly textured surface. A yarn may be very fine or it may be bulky, in which case it will knit up quickly. Novelty yarns have the advantage of not requiring fancy stitches to showcase them. You can easily produce beautiful fabrics with very plain knitting, and these yarns are forgiving of uneven gauge, which means the new knitter can let the yarn do all the work.

Knitting yarns are typically sold in balls and skeins and occasionally on cones. The ball bands on commercially produced yarns will give you a great deal of information. They'll tell you what the yarn is composed of and give you an indication of the gauge you can expect to obtain. Suggested needle sizes are usually given, as well as care instructions for the particular yarn. Always buy enough yarn to complete your project, as the yarn may not be available in the same dye lot later or may even be completely sold out. Unused balls can usually be returned to the yarn shop or put into your yarn stash for future use.

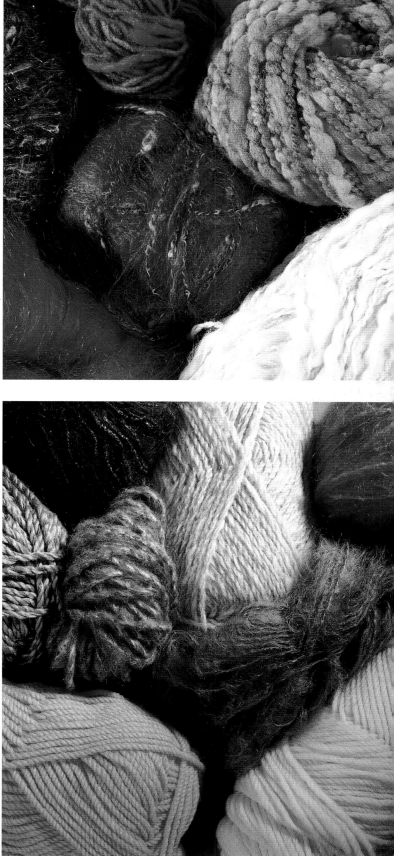

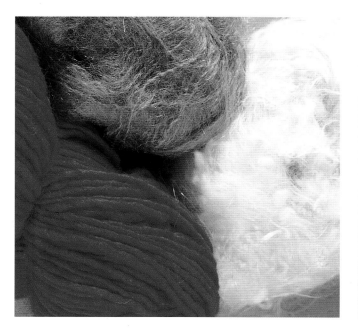

Winding Yarns

Many yarns today are sold as hanks. These need to be rewound into a ball before you begin to knit. There are a number of ways to do this. You can use the time-honored method of enlisting the nearest available helper to hold the skein, which you drop over his or her (hopefully willingly) outstretched hands. Or, you can hang it over the back of a chair, a door knob, your knees, or a pulled-out drawer. You can also, of course, use one of the beautiful skein winders made for this purpose. You simply adjust it to hold the hank and then wind the yarn off slowly, either onto a ball winder or onto a handmade ball. Take care when arranging the hank that all the yarn strands are lying correctly and smoothly, or they will tangle. It's a good idea not to untie the hank until everything is lined up correctly. Hanks may have a mind of their own. When they're difficult, I sometimes find it easier to wind a ball first just to "tame" the yarn, then rewind it into a nice, inviting ball. Do keep everything loose and relaxed during this process—and that includes you! If you pull, the yarn tightens up and may tangle. Even if this should happen, don't get frustrated, but keep it loose, wind slowly, slowly, and gently unravel the knots.

And by the way, why not display your gorgeous hanks of yarn in a suitable container while they await their chance to be of service?

Making and Measuring a Gauge Swatch

This preparation step is of the utmost importance—unless you really enjoy unpleasant surprises. It's rather like test-driving a car. You need to see how the yarn behaves, how it feels in your hands, and what results you can expect from it. Once you've selected the yarn and needles, cast on a minimum of 20 stitches—preferably more—and knit a swatch of at least 4 inches (10 cm). Before you measure it, handle the piece to decide if it feels good enough against the skin to wear comfortably. Does it have the right "hand" for the item you're making? If you'll be washing the finished garment, you should ideally wash and dry the gauge swatch first. Then, lay your swatch down on a flat surface, place pins to indicate where you'll start measuring, and measure with a ruler, carefully counting the stitches in exactly 4 inches (10 cm). I like to use the sort of clear plastic ruler used by quilters.

Measure without stretching the knitting, and do not include the edge stitches, which easily distort. If your gauge differs from that given in your pattern by even a fraction of an inch, your finished piece may be significantly larger or smaller than it should be, which, of course, could be quite devastating. If your gauge swatch is too big, try again on smaller needles. Use bigger needles if your swatch is smaller than it should be.

Using Patterns and Schematics

Step-by-step instructions accompany every project in this book. Before you begin a project, it's a good idea to read through the pattern carefully to familiarize yourself with what you'll be doing.

Pattern instructions are usually given in a range of sizes. Determine which size you want to use, and mark it in some way to highlight your requirements. (If you don't want to mark the pattern itself, photocopy it, then mark it up. Photocopies are also useful so you don't have to carry the whole book around with you.) To determine your size, check the measurements given for the garment. For all sweaters, vests, and tops, the pattern is accompanied by a schematic, which is a diagram of the finished piece with all the measurements indicated. Do remember that even if your bust measurement is 34 inches (86 cm), the finished garment is unlikely to measure 34 inches (86 cm), unless you're knitting a second skin. All patterns have ease added to them. This extra width, which often surprises new knitters, provides wearing comfort. Measure your favorite loose-fitting sweater, and you'll likely find that it actually measures quite a bit more than you are accustomed to thinking of as your "size."

The schematic also gives finished lengths, so you can decide in advance if you want to adjust the body or sleeve lengths. It's a good idea to keep a record of any changes you make in case you want to knit the item again later. You should also note for future reference what gauge you achieve with a particular yarn.

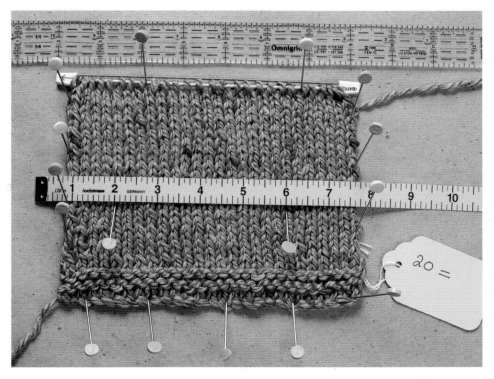

Measuring a gauge swatch

Substituting Yarns

Ideally, we'd all like to pick out a pattern and have the yarn it specifies readily available, but often this isn't the case. Experienced knitters know that some yarns may be available for a short time only. Manufacturers produce many new yarns each year; after all, they're in business to make money, so they need to offer different yarns regularly—and what a wonderful job they do of tempting us. The trouble is, when they offer new yarns, they discontinue others. There are other reasons a particular yarn might be difficult to find. Your own favorite yarn store, whether it be local or a mail-order business, can carry only so much, so it may simply not have the yarn you're looking for. Or, perhaps you live in a country where the yarn specified isn't available. Then again, maybe you've picked up the pattern years after its publication, and the yarn is long gone.

Even if you are able to find the yarn the pattern specifies, there are reasons you might want to use a different one. Perhaps you're allergic to the wool yarn it calls for, for example, or the cost of the yarn is an important consideration for you, as is the question of garment care. For some knitters, the ability to machine wash an item is crucial, so they want to substitute with a synthetic or machine-washable blend of fibers.

Certain basic yarns are easy to find, year in, year out, and most seasoned knitters have their favorites, be they baby yarns, smooth worsted weights, cabled cottons, or cuddly mohairs. Manufacturers and shop owners rely on the steady sales of these tried-and-true yarns, but for added excitement in knitting, it's hard to beat a new or different yarn that features that little something extra.

Whatever your reason for substituting one yarn for another, the undertaking is not at all difficult or mysterious, provided you follow this easy process.

• First, study the pattern. What is it that appeals to you? Frequently, color is the first thing we notice. Or, maybe it's the texture, a design detail, or the shape that catches your eye on a certain garment.

• Then, make sure the color, fiber, and texture of your substitution yarn will still achieve the look that attracted you to the design in the first place. You can do that by looking at a couple of factors:

  – Study the ball band. Look at the yardage (meters). This will tell you a great deal. Look at the recommended gauge. If your pattern calls for 5 sts to the inch (2.5 cm), and the ball band says it will knit to an ideal gauge of only 3 sts to the inch (2.5 cm), you can see at once that you might be getting into trouble.

  – Examine the texture; feel the "hand" of your proposed substitute yarn. Does the original design have a soft drape? Will your substitute yarn drape as well?

• If you're not sure of your choice, and particularly if the yarn is expensive, buy a ball and test it first. This isn't a waste of money should you decide not to use that yarn after all. You can put it to good use later (many of the projects in this book are ideal for using up odd balls), and you'll learn more about yarns and their properties. Yarn store owners usually knit swatches of the yarns to display for their customers. Handle these, and ask if there may be a tiny scrap of the yarn left over for you to test.

• Finally, do bear in mind that the finished article will not look exactly the same when you substitute a yarn. If you make an informed choice, though, you're likely to be pleased with the results.

Knit and Purl Stitches

Knit and purl are the two stitches on which all other stitches are based. Here's a refresher on the basics of each.

Knit

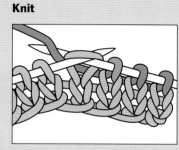

Insert the right needle into the first stitch of the left one, going from front to back.

Pass the yarn under and up the front of the right needle. Draw it through the stitch with the right needle.

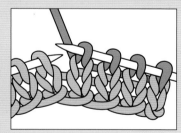

Drop the stitch from the left needle. The stitch on the right needle is your knit stitch.

Purl

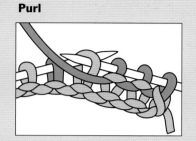

Position the yarn in the front of your work. Insert the right needle into the first stitch on the left needle, going from back to front.

Pass the yarn over, down the back, and under the right needle. Draw it through the stitch to the back.

Drop the stitch from the left needle. The stitch on the right is your purl stitch.

Casting On

There are many ways to cast on and create a foundation row for your knitting, and knitters soon start playing favorites. The two that are used most frequently are cable cast on and long-tail cast on.

CABLE CAST ON

Place a slipknot onto the needle, and knit one stitch into it.

Insert the right-hand needle between these two stitches, knit a stitch, and replace it on the left-hand needle.

Continue for the required number of stitches. This creates a firm edge with the look of a tiny cable, but it is not very elastic. It's a good cast on to use when you must add several stitches at the edge of a piece of knitting.

LONG-TAIL CAST ON

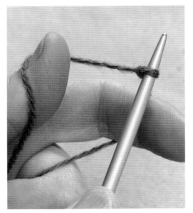

Leave a length of yarn (the long tail), make a slipknot, and put it on the right-hand needle. Position the yarn so that the tail end is over your left thumb, with the yarn from the ball over the left index finger. Hold the yarn in the palm of your hand with the other fingers.

Point the needle down toward your palm, and move it up through the loop on your thumb.

Then, move it over and under the yarn on your index finger.

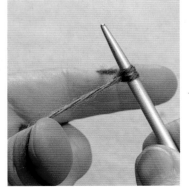

Remove your thumb from the loop, and use your thumb and index finger to tighten the stitch now placed on the needle. Repeat until you have the required number of stitches. You can use either side as the right side.

STOCKINETTE STITCH

You form this stitch by knitting alternate rows of knit and purl stitches. Stockinette stitch does not lie flat, but curls on all edges. You can use this feature, as I did in the Kid's Sweater, page 22, to enhance a design. This stitch has a very distinct right and wrong side, but the "wrong" side can sometimes be more attractive, especially if you're using a highly textured yarn, where the bumps are thrown to the back of the knitting. If the back of the knitting is the right side, it's called reverse stockinette stitch.

Stockinette stitch

Reverse stockinette stitch

GARTER STITCH

This is a knitter-friendly stitch! Every row in garter stitch is a knit row, and for every two rows knitted, one garter stitch ridge is formed, so it's easy to count the rows. It's a fully reversible stitch that doesn't curl at the edges, and its ability to lie flat makes it very useful.

CIRCULAR KNITTING

As the name suggests, knitting in this manner produces a seamless tube of knitted fabric, which you can work on a circular needle or on a set of double-pointed needles. (You may see instructions telling you to change from a circular needle to a set of double points when the stitches are decreased to the stage where they can no longer fit around the circular needle.) Circular knitting has a great many advantages. You cast the stitches onto the circular needle in the usual way, and then join them into a round. You must take care here to ensure that the stitches aren't twisted on the needle, then use the right-hand needle to knit the first stitch off the left-hand needle, pulling the stitches tightly together at the beginning of the round. You place a marker to indicate the beginning of the round—then round and round you go!

BINDING OFF

To secure your last row of knitting, you need to bind off. Work the first two stitches on the left-hand needle, then use the point of the left-hand needle to lift the first stitch on the right-hand needle over the second stitch. Knit the next stitch on the left-hand needle, and repeat the procedure. It's a good idea to use a larger needle when binding off, so you don't pull the stitches too tightly. Stitches are usually bound off in the pattern stitch. So for example, in k1p1 rib, you would knit and purl the stitches as they present themselves.

Three-Needle Bind Off

I use this technique wherever possible, since it's not only a great time saver, but it results in a less-bulky seam with a very neat appearance. It's a particularly useful method of binding off and simultaneously joining shoulder seams. Just as its name suggests, you use three needles. Arrange the two sets of stitches on the needles, with the right sides together, and bind off with a needle one size larger. The bind off is worked in the usual manner, except that you insert the needle into the first stitch on both the needles holding stitches.

Insert the third needle into the first stitch on each needle, and knit them together.

You have one stitch on the right-hand needle.

Insert the third needle into the next pair of stitches, and knit them together.

Pass the first stitch over the second.

INCREASING STITCHES

There are several ways to add a single stitch within your knitting. One of the simplest is to knit into the front and back of the same stitch. You can use this technique to make a decorative element within the work, while simultaneously shaping the knitting.

DECREASING STITCHES

As with increasing, many different methods exist to reduce the number of stitches on the needle. Two common decreases are the k2tog, which means knitting two stitches together and which slants to the right, and the ssk, which slants to the left and is worked by slipping the first stitch as if to knit, slipping the next stitch the same way, and then knitting the two stitches together through the backs of the loops.

> **NOTE:** When working increases and decreases, work these one or two stitches in from the edge(s) of the knitting. This gives a nice smooth edge to the work and makes seaming much easier.

Decreasing stitches: k2tog

Decreasing stitches: ssk

PICKING UP STITCHES

Sweater patterns may call for picking up stitches to place a finished edge on a knitted piece. Sleeve bands on vests, front edge bands on cardigans and jackets, and neckbands are examples. When you're picking up a large number of stitches, circular needles may be necessary, because they come in much longer lengths than straight needles.

Beautifully finished bands are not difficult to achieve if you follow a few simple steps. First, divide and mark the edges of the knitting where the stitches will be picked up into equal segments. Count the rows between the markers to ensure even spacing. (Safety pins work well as markers, because they won't fall out of the knitting.) With the right side facing you, carefully separate the edge stitches so that you can see the small space (or hole) between each row of knitting. Push the needle through the hole to the back of the work, then place the yarn around the needle as if to knit, and draw a loop of yarn through with the needle. Continue along the edge in this way, picking up the stitches at a ratio of two stitches for every three rows. (In other words, you'll miss every third space.) When you've picked up all the stitches, continue knitting the bands in the desired pattern stitch.

Remember that the number of stitches you end up with is dependent on the number of rows in the edge you're picking up from. You may end up with a different number of rows than called for in your instructions if you've changed the length of the piece or if your knitting style or yarn choice changed the row gauge.

It's difficult to see whether the stitches have been picked up evenly when they're bunched together on the needle. Unfortunately, some knitters don't check the fit of the garment before completing the finishing. It's very disappointing to find that the neckline fits poorly or that bands don't lie flat, and yet you can easily remedy this problem. Try this method to check the fit. Thread a bodkin with a thread in a contrasting color, and take the stitches carefully off the knitting needle. Adjust them evenly on this thread, so you can see how it will look when bound off. If you have too many stitches, your band will be wavy. If there are too few, it will pull in. Count the stitches and decide how many to add or remove. When you're satisfied, place the stitches back on the knitting needle and complete the bands.

BLOCKING

Blocking is the process of smoothing out the knitted pieces to the correct size and shape before you assemble them. I usually prefer the wet blocking method: it's simple, safe for all yarns, and always gives me good results. To block a piece of knitting, first pin it out to the correct shape, using blocking pins. The pins are made of stainless steel so they don't rust and are available at any good yarn shop. Position the pins at regular intervals all around the edges of the knitting, then check that the pieces are the correct size by comparing them to the schematic.

You'll need to work on a large, flat surface. Blocking boards designed for this purpose are available, or you can work on the floor with a towel under the knitting. Once your pieces are pinned out, spray them lightly with water and leave the knitting to dry. It's amazing how this improves the look of the knitting.

SEAMING

Your goal is to achieve a beautiful seam, and with a little care, you'll do just that, even if you don't ordinarily spend a lot of time with a sewing needle. In most cases you'll work the seams with the same yarn you use for the knitting, but when the yarn is too textured to use easily, choose a smooth matching yarn (see the Strappy Little Bag, page 75). Use a bodkin or a tapestry needle for seaming, and pin the seams together, if necessary, with knitter's pins. These are long and have a large head, so they don't disappear into the knitted fabric. Avoid working with a long length of yarn, as the friction may cause the yarn to break or fray.

Mattress Stitch

Mattress stitch is an excellent, all-purpose seaming stitch, resulting in an invisible seam. It's always worked with the right side of the work facing you, making it very easy to match stripes. To sew a seam in mattress stitch, first place the two pieces of knitting to be joined on a flat surface. Thread the needle and work upward one stitch in from the edge, passing the needle under the bar between the first and second rows on one side of the knitting, and then moving to the corresponding rows on the other side. Pick up two bars and return to the first piece, going into the knitting at the same point you came out, and pick up two bars. Repeat these steps, working from side to side and pulling the seam closed as you go, taking care not to pull so tightly that you cause puckers. You want a flat, neat seam.

When seaming reverse stockinette pieces, use the same method, but take only one bar at a time for better seam control.

MAKING BOBBLES

These are very useful embellishments on knitwear. They can be knitted in as the work is progressing or added later. Brightly colored bobbles are a great way to enliven an otherwise plain sweater, while same-colored bobbles lend texture and elegance to knitted pieces. The size of a bobble will vary, depending on the thickness of the yarn and the number of stitches you use.

To knit a bobble:

Cast on one stitch, leaving a length of yarn to secure the bobble with, then k1, p1, k1, p1 into the stitch (5 sts).

Work 4 rows in St st.

Cut the yarn, thread it through a tapestry needle, and draw up tightly through the sts.

Fasten the bobble firmly into position.

Fit to Knit

Do remember to take breaks from your knitting to stretch your muscles and loosen up; this is particularly important if you're knitting while a passenger on a long trip. Here are some general knitter-care tips.

- Keep your posture relaxed
- Avoid gripping the needles
- Try to keep the knitting in your lap, so your arms aren't raised up in front of your face, which puts strain on your shoulders and back
- Every half hour or so, do some simple stretching exercises:
  - Swing your arms in a circular motion
  - Try stretching your arms above your head or out in front of you, with your fingers interlaced
  - Wiggle your fingers and wrists
  - Hunch your shoulders up to your ears and relax again
  - Put your arms behind your back and grasp your elbows
  - Hug yourself

You can do many of these simple stretches even while sitting for long periods in a car. Finally, don't forget to care for your hands, and I don't just mean to use hand cream. Be easy on your hands. Too often, we use our hands for jobs that would be easier if we employed the right tool.

COMMON ABBREVIATIONS

Review the abbreviations in your pattern instructions to make sure you understand them.
If you're unsure about a particular technique, refer to a basic knitting text or ask a
knitting buddy to explain it to you.

*	repeat from * as many times as indicated
()	alternate measurement(s)/stitch counts
alt	alternate
approx	approximately
beg	begin or beginning
BO	bind off
cm	centimeter(s)
CO	cast on
cont	continued or continuing
dec	decrease or decreasing
g	gram
g st	garter stitch
inc	increase or increasing
k	knit
k2tog	knit two sts together
kg	kilogram
m	meter(s)
MC	main color
mm	millimeter(s)
N	needle
oz	ounces
patt	pattern
p	purl
rem	remain or remaining
rev St st	reverse stockinette stitch
RS	right side(s)
SC	single crochet
ssk	slip 1 st as if to knit, slip 1 st as if to knit, then knit these two sts tog, tbl
st(s)	stitch(es)
St st	stockinette stitch
tbl	through back of loop(s)
tog	together
WS	wrong sides
yds	yards
yfd	yarn forward
yrn	yarn round needle

KNITTING PROJECTS

Kid's Sweater

This is a bright, appealing sweater for a special child, but don't overlook the design opportunities in the eye-catching pattern stitch. You can very easily use the idea elsewhere—such as on a simple adult sweater or a hat.

YOU WILL NEED

Main color (MC): approximately 200 (270, 380, 450) yards (180, 243, 342, 405 m) of a chunky-weight yarn

Contrast colors (CC): small amounts in three colors (or as many as you like!)

Knitting needles in sizes 10 and 9 US (6 and 5.5 mm), or size necessary to achieve correct gauge

GAUGE

14 sts = 4 inches (10 cm); 3½ sts = 1 inch (2.5 cm)

FINISHED MEASUREMENTS

Chest: 24 (26, 28, 30) inches (61, 66, 71, 76 cm)

Length: 10½ (13, 15½, 17½) inches (27, 33, 39, 44.5 cm)

The weight of the yarn type I used is usually described as *chunky*. There are many different brands available in a wide range of colors and fiber combinations. As these yarns are sold in balls/skeins of different weights, I've given the quantities required for the sweater in yards (meters). You'll find this information on the ball band. The design is ideal for using up oddments. Or, buy some new yarn and make a number of sweaters in various stripe combinations. I've given precise instructions for the color work on the body of the sweater, but you are the designer for the sleeves. If you like, you can repeat the sequence already given. But why not do your own creative thing? You're sure to be delighted with the results.

MAKING THE BACK

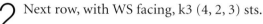

2 Next row, with WS facing, k3 (4, 2, 3) sts.

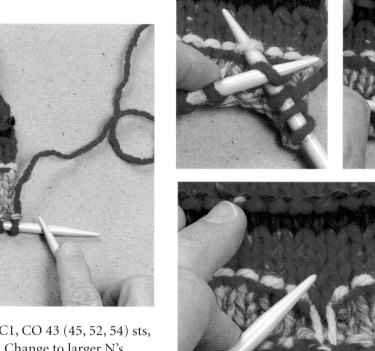

1 Using smaller N's and CC1, CO 43 (45, 52, 54) sts, and work 4 rows in St st. Change to larger N's. With CC2 and RS facing, knit 4 rows (2 g st ridges). With MC, work 7 rows in St st. Next row, with WS facing and CC1, knit 2 rows. With MC, work 4 rows in St st. Next row, with WS facing and CC2, knit 1 row. Join CC3 and work 6 rows in St st. Next row, with RS facing and MC, purl 1 row.

3 Insert N into the next st as if to knit, and then into the CC2 loop 7 rows below, and knit the 2 sts tog, knit 5, and pick up the loop below the next st in the same way as before. Continue like this across the row. This is not as difficult as it sounds! Look at the photos, and you'll see how the pulled-up sts are formed.

4 In the next row, we'll adjust the number of sts.
Next row:
1st size: dec 1 st (42).
2nd size: inc 1 st (46).
3rd and 4th sizes: dec 2 sts (50, 52).

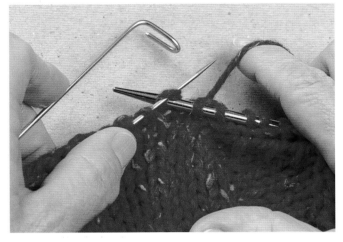

5 Continue working in St st until the back measures 10½ (13, 15½, 17½) inches (27, 33, 39, 44.5 cm) from the beg. BO 14 (15, 15, 15) sts, place the center 14 (16, 20, 22) sts on a holder, and BO the remaining 14 (15, 15, 15) shoulder sts.

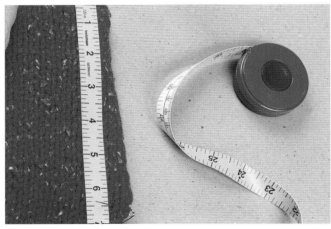

6 Place markers for the underarms 4½ (5½, 6½, 7) inches (11, 14, 16.5, 18 cm) from the top of shoulders.

MAKING THE FRONT

7 Work as given for the back until the piece measures 8½ (10½, 13, 14½) inches (22, 27, 33, 37 cm) from the beg.

SHAPING THE NECKLINE

8 With the RS facing, knit 26 (28, 31, 33), and place the next 16 (18, 19, 19) sts on a holder. Dec 1 st at the neck edge, working the decreases 1 st in from the edge on every other row until 14 (15, 15, 15) sts remain. Work straight until the piece measures the same as the back. BO the shoulder sts.

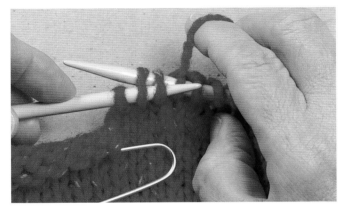

9 Return to the sts on the holder, leave the center 10 (10, 12, 14) sts on the holder, replace the remaining 16 (18, 19, 19) sts on the needle, and complete the neck shaping to match the first side, reversing all shapings.

MAKING THE SLEEVES

10 Using smaller N's and a color of your choice, CO 24 (26, 28, 30) sts, and work in the color and pattern stitch you like. At the same time, inc 1 stitch at each side every 4 rows until there are 32 (38, 46, 50) sts. Work straight until the sleeve measures 7 (8, 9, 11) inches (18, 20, 23, 28 cm) (or your required length) from the beg. BO the sts.

MAKING THE NECKBAND

11 Seam one shoulder. With smaller N's and a color of your choice, pick up approximately 44 (54, 60, 70) sts around the neck edge, including the sts left on the holders. Work 8 rows in St st. BO loosely.

FINISHING THE SWEATER

12 Seam the second shoulder and the neckband. Sew the sleeves in place between the markers. Join the side and sleeve seams, carefully matching the stripes. Darn in any loose ends.

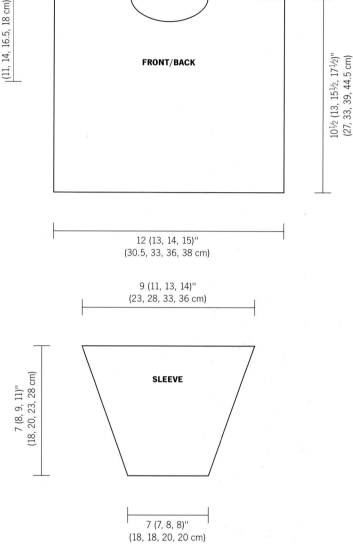

4 (4½, 4½, 4½)"
(10, 11, 11, 11 cm)

4 (4, 5, 6)"
(10, 10, 13, 15 cm)

4 (4½, 4½, 4½)"
(10, 11, 11, 11 cm)

FRONT/BACK

4½ (5½, 6½, 7)"
(11, 14, 16.5, 18 cm)

10½ (13, 15½, 17½)"
(27, 33, 39, 44.5 cm)

12 (13, 14, 15)"
(30.5, 33, 36, 38 cm)

9 (11, 13, 14)"
(23, 28, 33, 36 cm)

SLEEVE

7 (8, 9, 11)"
(18, 20, 23, 28 cm)

7 (7, 8, 8)"
(18, 18, 20, 20 cm)

Kid's Vest

Here's a comfortable, practical top to be worn on its own or layered with other garments. The checked border gives it a certain sophistication, and the knitting is easy. There are only two pieces and little finishing. Choose your colors, select a size, and you're off!

Approximately 280 (310, 370, 400) yards (252, 279, 333, 360 m) of a chunky-weight yarn (In addition, you'll need small amounts of black and white yarns.)

Knitting needles in sizes 8 and 9 US (5 and 5.5 mm), or size necessary to achieve correct gauge

GAUGE

16 sts = 4 inches (10 cm), measured over St st on larger needles

FINISHED MEASUREMENTS

Chest: 27 (28, 30, 32) inches (69, 71, 76, 81 cm)

Length: 14½ (15½, 17½, 19½) inches (37, 39, 44.5, 49.5 cm)

MAKING THE BACK

NOTE: When working with two colors, strand the yarn loosely across the back of the work.

1 Using smaller N's and black yarn (B), CO 54 (58, 58, 62) sts, and work 2 rows in k1p1 rib. Join in the white yarn (W), and work as follows:
Row 1: (k2W, k2B) to last 2 sts, k2W.
Row 2: (p2W, p2B) to last 2 sts, p2W.
Row 3: (k2B, k2W) to last 2 sts, k2B.
Row 4: (p2B, p2W) to last 2 sts, p2B.
Rows 5 and 6: repeat rows 1 and 2.
Cut the white yarn.

2 Using B, knit 4 rows (2 g st ridges). For the third and fourth sizes only, inc 1 st at each end of the next row (54, 58, 60, 64) sts.

3 Change to larger N's and your main yarn color, and work in St st until your piece measures 8½ (9, 10½, 12) inches (22, 23, 27, 30.5 cm) from the beg, ending with the RS facing.

4 CO 5 sts at the beg of the next 2 rows (64, 68, 70, 74) sts.

FINISHING THE VEST

5 Continue working in St st, knitting the first and last 5 sts of each row, until the back measures 13 (14, 16, 18) inches (33, 36, 41, 46 cm) from the cast-on edge, ending with the WS facing. Next row: k5, p13 (15, 15, 17), k28 (28, 30, 30), p13 (15, 15, 17), k5. Knit the following row. Repeat these 2 rows once, and then the first of these 2 rows again. The RS will now be facing.

WORKING THE BACK NECK AND SHOULDERS

6 Knit 21 (23, 23, 25), leave these sts on a holder, BO 22 (22, 24, 24), knit 21 (23, 23, 25). Next row: WS will be facing, k5, p13 (15, 15, 17), k3. Continue working on these shoulder sts until the back measures 14½ (15½, 17½, 19½) inches (37, 39, 44.5, 49.5 cm) from the cast-on edge, maintaining the g st edges.

BO the sts. Complete the other shoulder to match.

MAKING THE FRONT

7 Work as given for the back until the piece measures 11½ (12½, 14, 16) inches (29, 32, 36, 41 cm) from the beg, and then work the front neck and shoulder shaping as given for the back, completing the piece to match the back in length.

8 Join the shoulder seams. Sew the underarm and side seams, taking care to match the patterned borders.

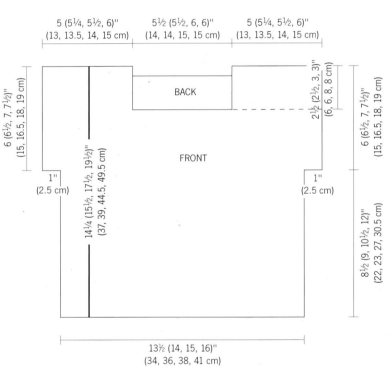

5 (5¼, 5½, 6)" (13, 13.5, 14, 15 cm) 5½ (5½, 6, 6)" (14, 14, 15, 15 cm) 5 (5¼, 5½, 6)" (13, 13.5, 14, 15 cm)

BACK

FRONT

6 (6½, 7, 7½)" (15, 16.5, 18, 19 cm)

14¼ (15½, 17½, 19½)" (37, 39, 44.5, 49.5 cm)

1" (2.5 cm)

2½ (2½, 3, 3)" (6, 6, 8, 8 cm)

6 (6½, 7, 7½)" (15, 16.5, 18, 19 cm)

1" (2.5 cm)

8½ (9, 10½, 12)" (22, 23, 27, 30.5 cm)

13½ (14, 15, 16)" (34, 36, 38, 41 cm)

Button-Up Hat

This cheerful hat takes very little yarn, plus it's quick to knit and a delight to trim with any of the wonderful variety of buttons available. Change colors as you please—the more, the merrier—and personalize a hat or two for a lucky youngster. Making several of these hats is also a great way to reduce your yarn and button collections.

YOU WILL NEED

For all sizes, you need a total of 1¾ oz (50 g) worsted-weight yarn

Knitting needles in size 8 US (5 mm), or size necessary to achieve correct gauge

Buttons, your choice

GAUGE

5 sts = 1 inch (2.5 cm), measured over St st

SIZES

Small (medium and large) (14, 16, 18 inches [36, 41, 46 cm])

MAKING THE BASIC HAT

1 Using a color of your choice, CO 72 (82, 92) sts, and work 1½ inches (4 cm) in St st.
Next row: (WS facing) knit.
Rows 1-7: work in St st.
Row 8: (WS facing) knit.
Repeat these 8 rows once more.
Continue in St st until the piece measures 4 (4½, 5) inches (10, 11, 13 cm) from the cast-on edge.

SHAPING THE CROWN

2 Row 1: k1, *k5 (6, 7), k2tog*, repeat to last st, k1.
Row 2 and every alt row: purl.
Row 3: k1, *k4 (5, 6), k2tog*, repeat to last st, k1.
Continue dec 10 sts this way on every knit row until there are 20 sts on the N. Purl 1 row. Next row, RS facing, k2tog across the row. 10 sts remain.

3 Cut the yarn, thread a tapestry needle, draw up the sts tightly, and fasten off securely.

FINISHING THE HAT

4 Sew up the center back seam, reversing the seam on the rolled edge. Darn in the yarn ends. Sew buttons on as desired.

Dingly Dangly Hat

You knit this quick and easy hat in only one piece. The design makes good use of yarn oddments, and the streamers are great fun.

YOU WILL NEED

Worsted weight yarn, about 100 yds (90 m)

Knitting needles in sizes 6 and 8 US (4 and 5 mm), or size necessary to achieve correct gauge

Buttons, if desired

GAUGE

5 sts = 1 inch (2.5 cm), measured over St st on larger needles

SIZES

Small (medium and large)

MAKING THE BASIC HAT

1 Using the color of choice and smaller N's, CO 40 (44, 48) sts. Work in k1p1 rib for 2 inches (5 cm), or work 4 inches (10 cm) if you want to fold back the ribbing.

2 Change to larger N's and another color of your choice, and work in St st for 4 (5, 6) inches (10, 13, 15 cm), ending on the wrong side.

3 Knit 1 row, thus making 1 g st ridge, which forms the fold line. Use a different color here if you like (see below).

4 Continue in St st for 4 (5, 6) inches (10, 13, 15 cm). Change to smaller N's, and work in rib as before. Bind off loosely in rib.

FINISHING

5 Block the knitting lightly. Fold the hat in half at the fold line, and sew side seams, reversing the seam on the last 2 inches (5 cm) of rib if this is to be folded back.

MAKING THE STREAMERS

6 With smaller N's and any yarn, CO 20 sts and cast them off again.

7 Attach the streamers to the hat, as shown.

A NOTE ON STREAMERS: The length of the streamers is your choice. The more stitches you cast on, the longer they'll be. Make them in many colors, or try making them all one color in varied lengths.

Baby Socks

These adorable socklets are nothing more than tubes. They're quick and easy to knit; you can complete a pair in an evening, making them an ideal last-minute gift. A few yards or meters of yarn are all you need, so put the tiniest scraps to good use, and knit some bright and cheerful socks to delight any baby.

MAKING THE BASIC SOCK

1 Using a color of your choice and smaller N's, CO 20 sts and work 1½ inches (4 cm) of k1p1 rib. Continue working in St st with the larger N's until the piece measures 5 inches (13 cm) from the beg.

2 Shape the toe. With the RS facing: k1, ssk, knit to last 3 sts, k2tog, k1.

Next row: purl.
Repeat these two rows until 12 sts remain. BO, and make a second piece the same way.

FINISHING THE SOCK

3 Sew the two pieces of the sock together, and embellish them as you like.

Variations

There are as many variations as your yarn stash and imagination allow. Use variegated yarns, knit stripes, work the ribbings in stripes, make the sole in a different color, decorate with multi-colored bobbles, make pairs of socks with the stripes and/or colors reversed, or make wildly colored, mismatched pairs.

BEE SOCK

1 Work the sole of the sock in black yarn.

2 For the top, work the ribbing in yellow, and continue in St st as for the basic sock, working 2 rows yellow, 2 rows black.

3 For the wings, CO 3 sts in yellow, and knit one row. Row 1: k1, inc1, k1, inc1, k1 (5 sts).

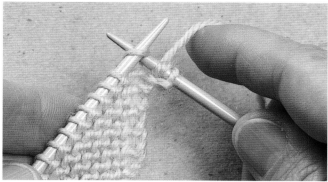

4 For the next row and every alt row: knit.

Row 3: work as row 1 to the end of the row (9 sts).
Row 5: k1, inc1, k3, inc1, k1, inc1, k3, inc1, k1 (13 sts).
Row 7: k1, inc1, k5, inc1, k1, inc1, k5, inc1, k1 (17 sts).
Row 9: k1, inc1, k7, inc1, k1, inc1, k7, inc1, k1 (21 sts).
Knit 1 row.

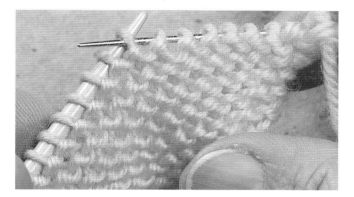

5 Break off the yarn, leaving an end. Thread a tapestry needle, and draw the yarn through the sts to fasten off.

6 Attach the wings as shown.

7 Using black yarn, crochet a short chain. Thread through a large-eyed needle, and attach it in the middle of the wings. Tie a knot at each end of the chain.

8 For the eyes, make two bobbles in yellow, and attach them firmly, as shown.

FLOWER SOCK

1 For the frill, using smaller N's, CO 40 sts and knit 6 rows (3 g st ridges). Knit 2 tog to the end of the row (20 sts). Continue as for the basic sock, changing colors as desired.

2 Make a flower (two parts) by casting on 40 sts using smaller needles.
Row 1: knit.
Row 2: purl.
Row 3: k2tog to end (20 sts).
Row 4: purl.
Repeat rows 3 and 4 once (10 sts) and row 3 once more.

3 Draw yarn through the remaining 5 sts, pull tightly, and fasten off. Make a second part (in a different shade if you like), arrange the two parts of the flower on the sock, and sew them firmly in place. Crochet a short chain or use a length of yarn and tie it in the middle of the flower.

BOBBLE SOCK

Make the basic sock, and decorate it with bobbles (see page 19). Attach them firmly to the sock.

If you like, crochet a chain or thread a ribbon through the sock to fasten the socks securely onto active little feet.

GoogliBug

This lovable knitted creature is for kids of all ages. Because the design happily accommodates any mix of colors and weights of yarn, it's a wonderful way to use up your oddments. If you make GoogliBug in a heavier or a fluffier yarn, using suitably larger needles, he'll willingly respond and become bigger. If you knit Googli on finer needles, using a fingering-weight yarn, he'll be much smaller and can cheerfully accompany you around on your key chain. If you want your GoogliBug to be longer than the Googli featured here, just give him extra segments.

Yarns of choice

Knitting needles of the appropriate size

A small amount of stuffing

The basic GoogliBug uses very little yarn, thus giving you a good opportunity to reduce the odds and ends in your yarn collection. Even the tiniest scrap can be used to embellish Googli. If you anticipate that your GoogliBug will be washed, choose your materials accordingly.

GAUGE

The gauge will depend on your yarn choice, but don't knit too loosely.

SIZE

Anything! The orange and lilac GoogliBug shown here is 13 inches (33 cm) from his head to the start of his tail. He was knitted in worsted-weight yarn.

MAKING THE BASIC GOOGLIBUG

1 CO 6 sts.
Row 1: k1 (inc1, k1) to end (11 sts).
Row 2: purl.
Repeat rows 1 and 2 twice more (41 sts).
Continue knitting in St st until you have the body length you want. Change colors as you like.

MAKING THE TAIL

2 With the RS facing, begin the decreases:
Row 1: k3, k2tog (k2, k2tog) to end of row (31 sts).
Next and every other row: purl.
Row 3: k2, k2tog (k1, k2tog) to end of row (21 sts).
Row 5: k1, (k2tog) to end of row (11 sts).
Row 7: as row 5 (6 sts).
Row 9: k2tog to end (3 sts).
Row 11: k3tog.

3 Don't draw the yarn through this remaining stitch.
Using the remaining stitch, CO 25 sts with the cable cast on method.

4 Cast the sts off again.

5 Cut the yarn, draw it tightly through the remaining st, and fasten off firmly. Tie a knot at the base of the tail.

FINISHING GOOGLIBUG

6 At the head end, weave the cast-on yarn tail through the cast-on sts, and pull up tightly. Fasten off.

7 Sew up the body, with the WS facing. Sew a little at a time, using a baseball stitch and stuffing lightly as you work.

8 Cut double lengths of yarn, and tie them tightly around the body to form segments. Bury the yarn ends.

Now the real fun begins, as GoogliBug takes on his personality. Remember that Googli likes to be different, so adorn him any way you like.

MAKING THE NOSE

Knit a fat bobble (see page 19), and attach it to the face.

MAKING THE EYES

Make bobbles or embroider French knots.

MAKING THE FEELERS

CO 12 sts and bind them off again, then sew them in place. Or, crochet short chains, attach them to the head, and tie a knot at the end of each chain.

MAKING THE FEET

CO 6 sts, and cast them off again. Make as many as you like, and attach them in pairs.

Admire your handiwork, then make GoogliBug a companion or two!

Top-Notch Hat

A perky little hat like this will brighten up any chilly day. Mohair
yarns are so luxurious and come in a wonderful array of colors.
Do you need an excuse to fill a hatbox with several of these?

2 balls of Classic Elite La Gran Mohair, 1½ oz (42 g) = 90 yds (81 m)

Knitting needles in sizes 9 and 10.5 US (5.5 and 7 mm),
or size necessary to achieve correct gauge

GAUGE

3 sts = 1 inch (2.5 cm), measured over St st with larger needles

SIZE

To fit the average adult head

MAKING THE HAT

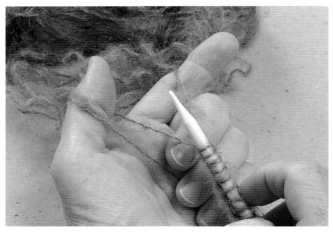

1 Using the smaller N's, CO 70 sts and work 1½ inches (4 cm) in St st. Change to larger N's, and continue in St st until the work measures 8 inches (20 cm) from the beg.

2 Begin shaping the top:
1st dec row: k1 (k2tog, k1) to the end of the row (47 sts).
Knit a further 2 inches (5 cm).

3 2nd dec row: k1 (k2tog) to the end of the row (24 sts).
Work a further 10 inches (25 cm) on these 24 sts.

4 Bind off.

FINISHING

5 Sew up the center back seam, reversing the seam at the rolled edge.

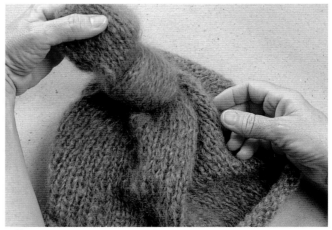

6 Darn in the yarn ends neatly, and tie a saucy knot as shown.

Knotted Scarf

This scarf could not be any easier to knit. It's nothing more than a long strip of stockinette with a knot tied at each end, and it's designed to roll in on itself. You could make a whole wardrobe of these, in all manner of colors, so why limit yourself? Give a few as gifts, and you'll be top of the pops. For added interest, scatter a few beads here and there.

FINISHING

3 Darn in the yarn ends neatly.

MAKING THE SCARF

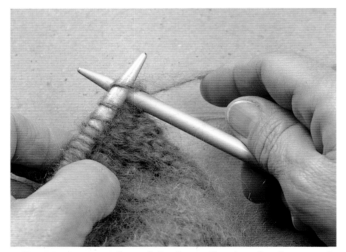

1 CO 30 sts and work in St st, slipping the first st of every row.

2 Continue knitting until there is enough yarn left to BO, loosely.

4 Tie a knot at each end of the scarf, and flare the ends of the scarf out.

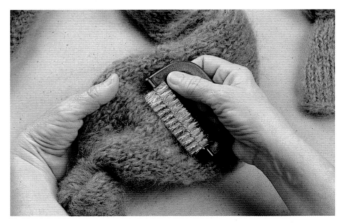

5 Use a mohair brush, if you like, to fluff up the yarn's pile. Fling the scarf artfully about your neck, and dazzle the world!

Where Did You Get That Hat?

The beauty of this hat is that the novelty yarn does all the work, so you can let your imagination run wild. It's a good excuse to buy just one ball of that fabulous but pricey novelty yarn you've had your eye on, or to snap up a ball or two from the sale bin. It's also so quick and easy, you can make it in an evening. Your choice of yarn will determine the size and appearance of your hat. A very dense yarn will result in a fatter hat; a lofty yarn will give you a softer one. And if you decide you don't want to wear the hat yourself, it's a perfect addition to your gift stash.

• The following instructions are written for knitting the hat in the round, but you may, if you prefer, knit it flat. If you do that, add one stitch at each end, to be used for the seam. Just remember that you won't see a reference to these two added stitches in the instructions. Work in stockinette stitch, and sew up the center back seam when you finish.

• The decreases for shaping the crown of the hat are very simple; the texture of the yarn will hide any mistakes.

A small amount of worsted-weight yarn that will knit to a gauge of 5 sts to the inch (2.5 cm)

About 65 yards (58.5 m) of a novelty yarn (A bulky yarn that will knit to approx 3 sts = 1 inch [2.5 cm] on St st is suitable.)

Knitting needles in size 7 (4.5 mm) for the worsted weight and in the appropriate size for your novelty yarn (Check your ball band for recommendations on needle size. You'll probably use needles in the size 10 (6 mm) range. If you're knitting in the round, you'll also need a set of double-pointed needles in the larger size. Change to these needles when you can no longer work comfortably on the circular needle.)

To fit the average adult head

MAKING THE HATBAND

1 Using the smaller circular needle and the worsted-weight yarn, CO 100 sts, and join them into a circle, being careful not to twist the sts. Mark the beginning of the round, and work in k1p1 rib for 1½ inches (4 cm).

70 w/size 8

2 Knit one round.

MAKING THE HAT

3 Change to the novelty yarn and the larger N, and knit 2 inches (5 cm).

SHAPING THE CROWN

4 1st dec round: (k2, k2tog) to the end of the round (75 sts). Work a further 2 inches (5 cm).
2nd dec round: (k2, k2tog) to last three sts, k1, k2tog (56 sts). Work a further 1 inch (2.5 cm).
3rd dec round: (k1, k2tog) to the last two sts, k2tog (37 sts).
Next round: knit.
4th dec round: k1 (k2tog) to end (19 sts).
Repeat the last two rows once (10 sts).

5 Cut the yarn, thread it through a tapestry needle, and draw up the sts tightly. Fasten off, and darn in any loose ends.

Place your yummy little hat in full view, and commence the next one. You'll be surprised how quickly you can have a whole basketful of these hats. Why not pop yarns suitable for hats into an attractive basket or other container and keep it in sight to inspire you?

Cravat-Style Scarf

One end of this little scarf is slotted through a buttonhole in the knitting, so it stays snugly in place, adding a touch of warmth and color at the throat. Make your first scarf in a basic yarn, then treat yourself to a more luxurious fiber, then try a different color, then make a gift…why stop at one?

YOU WILL NEED

About 130 yards (117 m) of a yarn that would typically give a gauge of 3½ or 4 sts to the inch (2.5 cm) over stockinette stitch. Choose a soft yarn with a little loft for the best results.

Check the information on your yarn's ball band to determine the appropriate needle size to use; you'll probably need needles in size 10 US (6 mm).

SIZE

Approximately 38 x 6 inches
(96.5 x 15 cm)

1 CO 24 sts loosely, and work in k2p2 rib for 8 inches (20 cm).

NOTE: Knit the first and last st of each row.

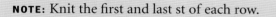

2 Begin making the buttonhole. Rib 12 sts, turn your work, and put the rem 12 sts on a holder. Work 2 inches (5 cm) on these sts, place them on another holder, cut the yarn, and return to the sts left on the holder.

3 Rejoin the yarn, and work to match the first side of the buttonhole. Arrange all the sts on the needle, and work across to close the buttonhole.

4 Continue knitting until the scarf is about 38 inches (96.5 cm) long, or the length you want. Bind off the sts in rib.

5 Darn in the yarn ends neatly. To wear your scarf, loop one end through the buttonhole.

VARIATION

Showcase an antique button or a handsomely carved ethnic one on a scarf like this to create a unique piece of neckwear. Adjust the finished scarf around your neck, mark the button placement with a pin, and sew it on. Button up. A word of warning: this can easily become addictive!

Classic Man's Hat

This rugged hat has a deep brim for extra warmth and casual good looks. Whether you knit it for him or he knits his own, this classic design is likely to be a hit.

MAKING THE HAT

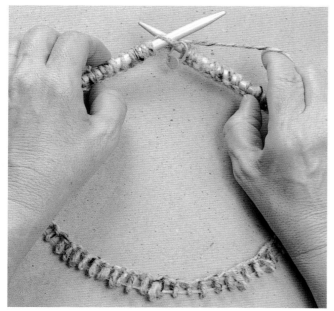

1 Using the smaller N, CO 72 sts, place a marker, and join into a round, being careful not to twist the stitches.

2 Work the pattern stitch as follows.
Rounds 1-4: (k4, p4), repeat to end of round.
Rounds 4-8: (p4, k4), repeat to end of round.
Repeat rounds 1-8 for approx 6 inches (15 cm), ending on a round 4 or 8.

3 Next row: k2tog, k34, k2tog, k34 (70 sts). Change to the larger N and knit in rounds for 2 inches (5 cm).

WORKING THE CROWN DECREASES

4 Change to the double-pointed needles when you have too few sts for the needle, as shown in the example here.
Round 1: (k8, k2tog) to end of round.
Round 2 and all even-numbered rounds: knit.
Round 3: (k7, k2tog) to end of round.
Round 5: (k6, k2tog) to end of round.
Round 7: (k5, k2tog) to end of round.
Round 9: (k4, k2tog) to end of round.
Round 11: (k3, k2tog) to end of round.
Round 13: (k2, k2tog) to end of round.
Round 15: (k1, k2tog) to end of round.
Round 17: k2tog to end of round.

5 Cut the yarn, thread it through the rem sts, and fasten off.

FINISHING

6 Darn in the yarn ends.

Classic Man's Scarf

A classic scarf like this is both elegant and practical.
This one features a good-looking tweed yarn.

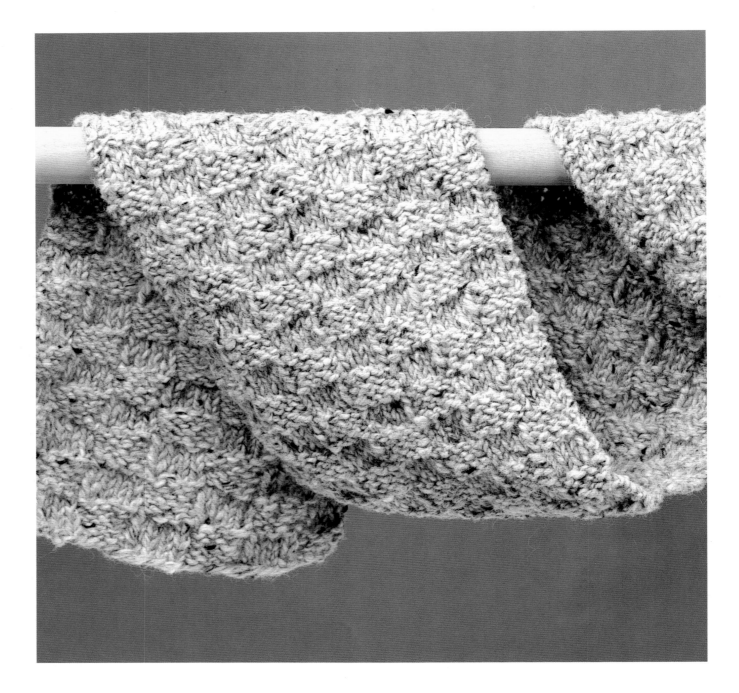

MAKING THE SCARF

1 CO 28 sts loosely, and work the 8-row pattern stitch as follows:

NOTE: Knit the first and last st of every row.

Row 1: (k4, p4) to last 4 sts, k4.
Row 2: (p4, k4) to last 4 sts, p4.
Rows 3 and 4: repeat rows 1 and 2.
Row 5: (p4, k4) to last 4 sts, p4.
Row 6: (k4, p4) to last 4 sts, k4.
Rows 7 and 8: repeat rows 5 and 6.

2 Repeat the pattern stitch until there is just sufficient yarn left to BO loosely, ending on row 4 or 8 of the pattern stitch.

FINISHING

3 Darn in the yarn ends.

NOTE: If you're making the hat that matches this scarf (see page 48), make it first. You should have some yarn left over, which you can use to make your scarf longer if you like.

Weekend Favorite

Every wardrobe needs a sweater like this—a comfy, cozy little number you can rely on to look good through your casual weekend activities. This type of yarn works well with your denims and cords.

MAKING THE BACK

1 Using the smaller N's, CO 50 (50, 54, 62) sts, and
establish the rib pattern as follows:
Row 1: k4, p1 (k3, p1) to last st, k1.
Row 2: k2 (p3, k1) to end of row.
Repeat these two rows for a total of 4 inches (10 cm).

2 Change to larger N's and work in St st, increasing
1 st at each end of the first row for the 2nd and 3rd
sizes only (50, 52, 56, 62) sts, until the piece measures
23 (23½, 24½, 26) inches (58, 60, 62, 66 cm).

3 With the RS facing, knit 18 (19, 20, 22) sts. Leave
rem sts on a holder. Purl 1 row. Dec 1 st at the
neck edge on the next row (17, 18, 19, 21) sts. Continue
in St st until the back measures 23½ (24, 25, 26½)
inches (60, 61, 63.5, 67 cm) from the beg. BO the
shoulder sts.

4 Rejoin the yarn to the sts on the holder. Knit
across 14 (14, 16, 18) sts, and place these on a
holder for the center back neck. Continue working on
the rem sts, and complete as for the first side, reversing
the shapings.

MAKING THE FRONT

5 Work as given for the back until the piece measures 20 (21, 22, 23) inches (51, 53, 56, 58 cm).

6 Begin shaping the neck. With the RS facing, knit
20 (21, 22, 24), and place the rest of the sts on a
holder. Dec 1 st at the neck edge every other row until
17 (18, 19, 21) sts remain. Work straight until the front

matches the back in length. BO the shoulder sts. Return to the sts on the holder, knit across 10 (10, 12, 14) sts, and place these on the holder for the center front neck.

7 Work on the rem sts, and complete the shoulder to match the first side, reversing the shapings.

KNITTING THE SLEEVES

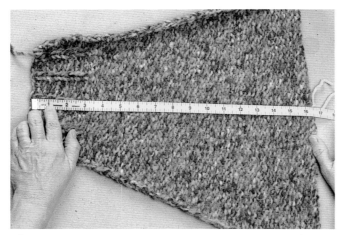

8 Using smaller N's, CO 22 (22, 26, 26) sts, and work in the rib pattern for 3 inches (8 cm). Change to larger N's and work in St st, inc 1 st on each side every 4 rows until there are 46 (48, 50, 56) sts on the N. Continue knitting until the sleeve measures 16½ (17, 17½, 17½) inches (42, 43, 44.5, 44.5 cm). Adjust the length, if necessary. BO loosely.

FINISHING THE SWEATER

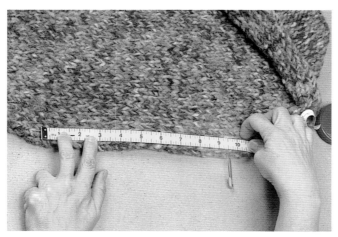

9 Block the pieces lightly. Seam the front and back together at one shoulder. Place markers 9 (9½, 10, 11) inches (23, 24, 25, 28 cm) down from the shoulders for the underarms on the back and front.

KNITTING THE NECKBAND

10 Using the smaller N's and with the RS facing, pick up and knit 50 (50, 54, 58) sts evenly around the neck, including the sts on holders. Work in the rib pattern for 1½ inches (4 cm). BO sts loosely.

NOTE: If you're knitting the neckband in the round, adjust the number of sts so that the rib pattern is uninterrupted.

11 Seam the rem shoulder and neckband sts. Sew the sleeves in place between the markers. Sew up the side and sleeve seams, taking care to match seams at the ribbed bands. Darn in any loose ends.

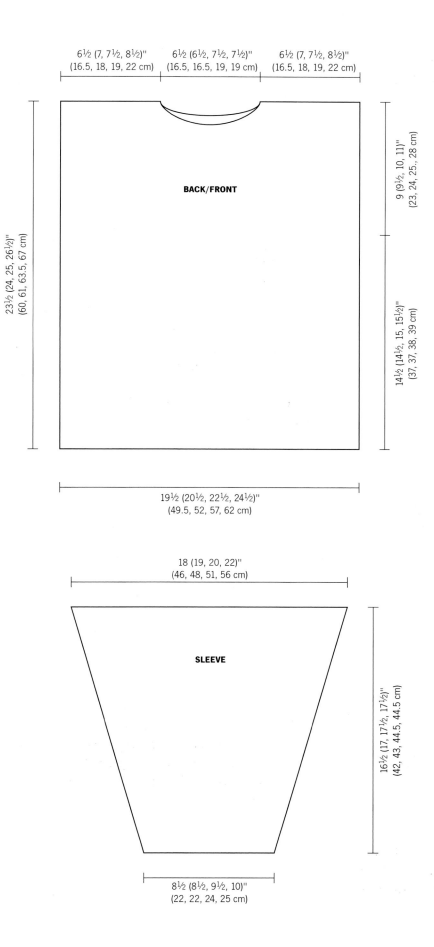

6½ (7, 7½, 8½)"
(16.5, 18, 19, 22 cm)

6½ (6½, 7½, 7½)"
(16.5, 16.5, 19, 19 cm)

6½ (7, 7½, 8½)"
(16.5, 18, 19, 22 cm)

BACK/FRONT

9 (9½, 10, 11)"
(23, 24, 25., 28 cm)

23½ (24, 25, 26½)"
(60, 61, 63.5, 67 cm)

14½ (14½, 15, 15½)"
(37, 37, 38, 39 cm)

19½ (20½, 22½, 24½)"
(49.5, 52, 57, 62 cm)

18 (19, 20, 22)"
(46, 48, 51, 56 cm)

SLEEVE

16½ (17, 17½, 17½)"
(42, 43, 44.5, 44.5 cm)

8½ (8½, 9½, 10)"
(22, 22, 24, 25 cm)

Rolled-Edge Sweater

The sleeve stitches of this sweater are picked up at the armhole, knitted to a flattering three-quarter length, and embellished with tiny buttons. The rolled edges add to the simple elegance of the design, which can take you through the day and into the evening.

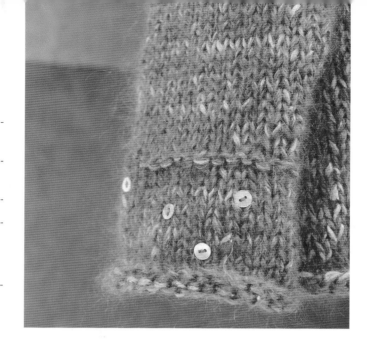

YOU WILL NEED

11 (11, 12, 13) hanks of Bravo by Classic Elite Yarns,
1¾ oz (50 g) = 48 yds (43 m)

Needles in sizes 10 and 10.5 US (6 and 7 mm),
or size necessary to achieve correct gauge

16-inch (41 cm) circular needle in
size 10 US (6 mm) (optional)

Small mother-of-pearl buttons

GAUGE

2.75 sts = 1 inch (2.5 cm)

SIZES

Small (medium, large, extra large)

FINISHED MEASUREMENTS

Bust: 39 (43, 47, 51) inches (99, 109, 119, 129.5 cm)

Length: 19 (20, 22, 23) inches (48, 51, 56, 58 cm)

Sleeve length: 13 inches (33 cm)

MAKING THE SWEATER BACK

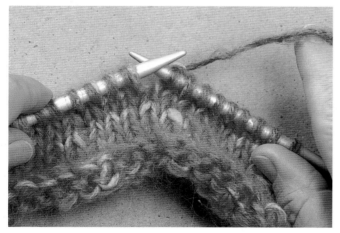

1 Using the smaller N's, CO 54 (60, 66, 70) sts, and work in St st for 1 inch (2.5 cm). Change to larger N's, and continue working in St st until the back measures 18 (19, 21, 22) inches (46, 48, 53, 56 cm) from the beg.

SHAPING THE BACK NECK AND SHOULDERS

2 With the RS facing, k19 (22, 24, 25) sts, and place the rem sts on a holder. Purl the next row. Dec 1 st at the neck edge on the following row. Work until the back measures 19 (20, 22, 23) inches (48, 51, 56, 58 cm) from the beg. Leave the rem 18 (21, 23, 24) shoulder sts on a holder.

3 Return to the unworked sts. Leave the center 16 (16, 18, 20) sts on the holder, place the rem shoulder sts back onto the N, and complete to match the first shoulder, reversing the shaping. Place markers on each side 9 (9½, 10, 10½) inches (23, 24, 25, 27 cm) from the top of the shoulder, to indicate the underarm.

MAKING THE FRONT

4 Work as given for the back until the piece measures 16 (17, 19, 19½) inches (41, 43, 48, 49.5 cm) from the cast-on edge.

SHAPING THE FRONT NECK AND SHOULDERS

5 With the RS facing, k20 (23, 25, 27) sts, and place the rem sts on a holder. Purl the next row. Dec 1 st at the neck edge on the next and every following alt row until 18 (21, 23, 24) sts rem. Work straight until the front matches the back in length. Leave the sts on a holder.

6 Return to the unworked sts. Leave the center 14 (14, 16, 16) sts on the holder, place the rem sts onto the needle, and complete to match, reversing the shapings.

WORKING THE NECKBAND

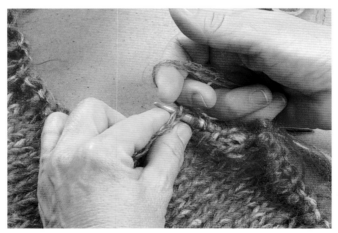

7 With the RS together, bind the shoulder sts off using the 3-needle BO. Using the circular N and with the RS facing, pick up and k9 (9, 10, 11) sts evenly along the left front neck. K14 (14, 16, 16) front neck sts from the holder, pick up and k9 (9, 10, 11) sts from the right front neck and a total of 20 (20, 22, 24) from the back neck (52, 52, 56, 62) sts. Work in St st for 1½ inches (4 cm). BO the sts loosely.

NOTE: If you prefer to knit the neckband on straight N's, BO one set of shoulder sts, then pick up the sts as given above, and work the neckband. Seam the second shoulder and the neckband, reversing the seam on the rolled edge.

KNITTING THE SLEEVES

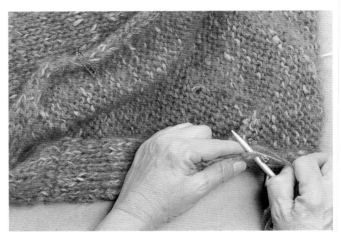

8 Using the larger N's pick up 50 (52, 54, 56) sts evenly between the markers and work in St st, dec 1 st on each side every 4 rows until there are 32 sts for all sizes. At the same time, when the sleeve is approx 9 inches (23 cm) long, with the WS facing, knit 1 row. Continue working in St st for a further 4 inches (10 cm) for all sizes. Adjust the sleeve length if necessary, then BO the sts.

FINISHING THE SWEATER

9 Sew up the side and sleeve seams, reversing the seams on the rolled edges. Block the knitting lightly. Sew on buttons as desired.

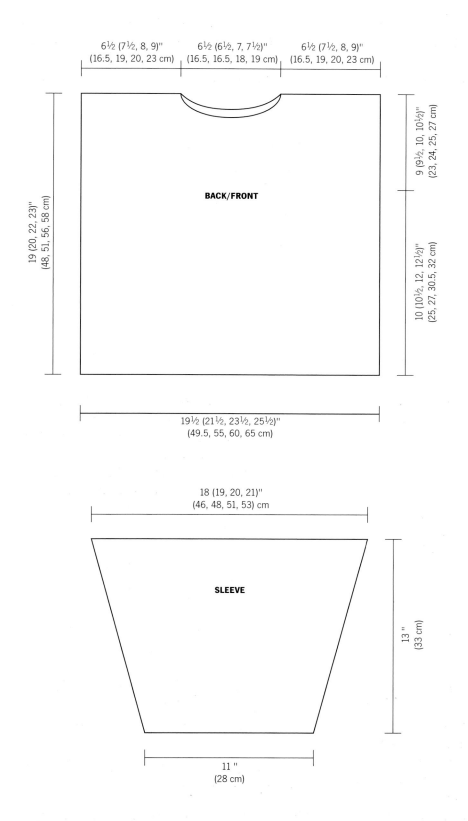

6½ (7½, 8, 9)"
(16.5, 19, 20, 23 cm)

6½ (6½, 7, 7½)"
(16.5, 16.5, 18, 19 cm)

6½ (7½, 8, 9)"
(16.5, 19, 20, 23 cm)

9 (9½, 10, 10½)"
(23, 24, 25, 27 cm)

BACK/FRONT

19 (20, 22, 23)"
(48, 51, 56, 58 cm)

10 (10½, 12, 12½)"
(25, 27, 30.5, 32 cm)

19½ (21½, 23½, 25½)"
(49.5, 55, 60, 65 cm)

18 (19, 20, 21)"
(46, 48, 51, 53) cm

SLEEVE

13 "
(33 cm)

11 "
(28 cm)

Tailored Vest

You'll work the armhole and button bands of this vest as the knitting progresses, so there's very little finishing to do before you can wear it. The knitting is so quick and easy, you'll be ready to make a wardrobe of vests to suit all your moods. Use the basic pattern for a tailored look. Shorten the length, switch to a brighter yarn, and perhaps add some embellishments for a sassier style. Or, make it much longer if you want a tunic-type vest.

4 (5, 5, 6) balls of Filatura di Crosa's Antibe, 1¾ oz (50 g) = 93 yds (84 m) (This is a softly brushed yarn that knits up into a very light fabric. Bear this in mind if you're looking for a substitute.)

Knitting needles in sizes 10 and 11 US (6 and 7 mm), or size necessary to achieve correct gauge

5 buttons

GAUGE

11 sts = 4 inches (10 cm);
2.75 sts = 1 inch (2.5 cm)

SIZES

Small (medium, large, extra large)

FINISHED MEASUREMENTS

Bust: 37 (40, 43, 48) inches
(94, 102, 109, 122 cm)

Length: 23½ (24, 25, 25½) inches
(60, 61, 63.5, 65 cm)

MAKING THE BACK

1 Using the smaller N's, CO 52 (54, 60, 66) sts, and knit 8 rows (4 g st ridges). Change to larger N's, and work in rev St st until the piece measures 14½ (14½, 15, 15½) inches (37, 37, 38, 39 cm) from the beg, ending with the RS facing. K8 (8, 9, 9) sts, purl to the last 8 (8, 9, 9) sts, and knit to the end. Next row: knit. Repeat these 2 rows once more.

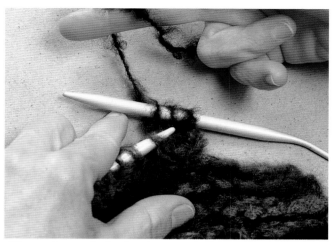

2 Begin armhole shaping. With the RS facing, BO 5 (5, 6, 6) sts, k3, purl to the last 8 (8, 9, 9) sts, and knit to the end. Next row: BO 5 (5, 6, 6) sts, and knit to the end. Continue working in rev St st, keeping 3 sts in g st at the armhole edges, until the back measures 23½ (24, 25, 25½) inches (60, 61, 63.5, 65 cm) from the beg. BO the sts.

MAKING THE LEFT FRONT

3 With smaller N's, CO 31 (32, 35, 38) sts, and knit 8 rows (4 g st ridges). Change to larger N's, and knit 1 row. Next row, RS facing, purl to the last 5 sts, k5. Continue working in rev St st, keeping 5 sts in g st at the left front edge until the piece matches the back to the start of the underarm shaping.

4 Begin armhole shaping. With the RS facing, BO 5 (5, 6, 6) sts, k3, purl to the last 5 sts, k5. Next row: knit.

5 Beg the dec for the neck shaping. K3, purl to the last 7 sts, p2tog, k5. Continue to dec 1 st at the neck edge every 4 rows until 19 (20, 22, 22) sts rem, remembering to keep 5 sts in g st at the neck edge and 3 at the armhole edge for the bands. Work straight until the front matches the back in length to the shoulder. BO 14 (15, 17, 17) sts, and continue knitting in g st on these rem 5 sts until the neckband is long enough to fit to the center back neck. Leave the sts on a holder.

6 Mark the positions of the buttons on the left front band, placing the first one ½ inch (1.5 cm) from the bottom and the last one ½ inch (1.5 cm) below the start of the neck shaping. Space the rest of the markers evenly in between. This is easy to do; just count the number of g st ridges.

MAKING THE RIGHT FRONT

7 Knit as for the left front, reversing all the shapings. At the same time, work the buttonholes to correspond with the markers.

FINISHING THE VEST

8 Join the shoulder seams. Adjust the length of the g st borders to meet at center back neck, and join them by weaving them together or with a 3-needle BO. Sew the border neatly in place along the back neck edge. Sew up the side seams. Sew on the buttons. Block the vest lightly. Sally forth blithely!

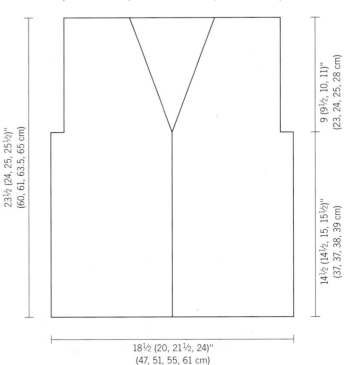

5 (5½, 6, 6½)" (13, 14, 15, 16.5 cm) 6½ (6½, 7, 7½)" (16.5, 16.5, 18, 19 cm) 5 (5½, 6, 6½)" (13, 14, 15, 16.5 cm)

9 (9½, 10, 11)" (23, 24, 25, 28 cm)

23½ (24, 25, 25½)" (60, 61, 63.5, 65 cm)

14½ (14½, 15, 15½)" (37, 37, 38, 39 cm)

18½ (20, 21½, 24)" (47, 51, 55, 61 cm)

Summer Shell

A useful piece in any wardrobe, you can wear this sleeveless top alone or under a jacket. We've chosen an interesting cotton novelty yarn in ice-cream colors, but a solid color or a smooth yarn would work equally well. Highly textured yarns like this one often have a very distinct appearance on the reverse, so you get to choose which side you want to present to the world. The neckline and armholes are finished in single crochet, which is quick and easy to do. For those who've never tried finishing knitwear this way, it's a good introduction to a useful technique.

MAKING THE BACK

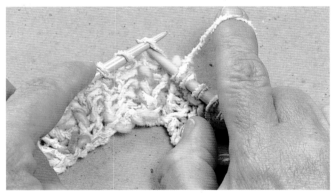

1 With smaller N's, CO 68 (76, 82, 90) sts, and work in k1p1 rib for 1½ inches (4cm). Change to larger N's, and work in St st until your work measures 12 (13, 13, 14) inches (30.5, 33, 33, 36 cm) from the beg.

2 To shape the armhole, BO 5 (6, 7, 8) sts at the beg of the next 2 rows 58 (64, 68, 74) sts.

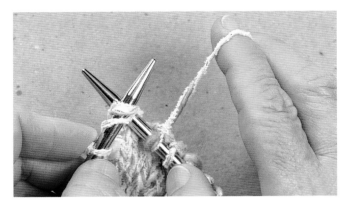

3 Dec 1 st at each side, working the dec 1 st in from the edge every other row 4 (6, 6, 7) times (50, 52, 56, 60) sts. Continue working on these sts until the work measures 17½ (18½, 19½, 20½) inches (44.5, 47, 49.5, 52 cm) from the beg.

WORKING THE BACK NECK SHAPING

4 With the RS facing, knit 13 (13, 15, 15) sts, BO the next 24 (26, 26, 30) sts, knit 13 (13, 15, 15) sts. Working each shoulder separately, dec 1 st at the neck edge every other row 2 times for all sizes 11 (11, 13, 13) sts. Leave the shoulder sts on holders.

MAKING THE FRONT

5 Work as for the back until the piece measures 14 (15, 15, 16) inches (36, 38, 38, 41 cm) from the beg.

WORKING THE FRONT NECK SHAPING

6 With the RS facing, k15 (15, 17, 18) sts, BO the next 20 (22, 22, 24) sts, k15 (15, 17, 18). Working each shoulder separately, dec 1 st at the neck edge every other row 4 (4, 4, 5) times (11, 11, 13, 13) sts. Continue working until the piece is the same length to the shoulders as the back. Leave the sts on holders.

FINISHING THE SHELL

7 With RS together, BO the shoulders, using a 3-needle BO.

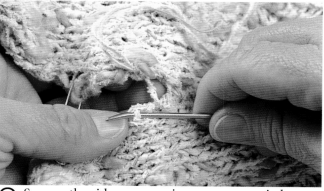

8 Sew up the side seams, using a mattress stitch.

9 With the RS facing, work a row of single crochet around the neckline and armholes.

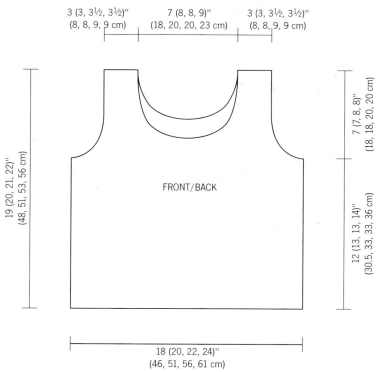

3 (3, 3½, 3½)" (8, 8, 9, 9 cm) 7 (8, 8, 9)" (18, 20, 20, 23 cm) 3 (3, 3½, 3½)" (8, 8, 9, 9 cm)

7 (7, 8, 8)" (18, 18, 20, 20 cm)

FRONT/BACK

19 (20, 21, 22)" (48, 51, 53, 56 cm)

12 (13, 13, 14)" (30.5, 33, 33, 36 cm)

18 (20, 22, 24)" (46, 51, 56, 61 cm)

Crop Top

This super-quick—not to mention sassy—knit requires little finishing, and the simple eyelet pattern stitch gives it a fresh appeal. If you prefer to make yours longer, remember to purchase extra yarn.

YOU WILL NEED

6 (6, 7, 8) balls of Berroco's Pronto 1¾ oz
(50 g) = 55 yds (50 m)

Knitting needles in size 10.5 US (6.5 mm),
or size necessary to achieve correct gauge

Crochet hook in size K/10.5 US (6.5 mm)

NOTE ON YARN SUBSTITUTION: If you use a different
yarn, choose a smooth yarn, so the eyelet pattern is
shown to advantage. A highly textured yarn will obscure
the pattern stitch.

GAUGE

13 sts = 4 inches (10 cm)

SIZES

Extra small (small, medium, large)

FINISHED MEASUREMENTS

Bust: 34 (36, 38, 40) inches (86, 91, 96.5, 102 cm)

Length: 17 (17½, 18 ½, 19) inches (43, 44.5, 47, 48 cm)

PATTERN STITCH

Row 1: (k2, yfd, k2tog) to end of row, k2.

Rows 2-6: work in St st.

MAKING THE BACK

1 CO 54 (58, 62, 66) sts, and work 4 rows in St st.
With the RS facing, work the 6-row pattern st a
total of 5 times for all sizes.

2 Continue in St st until the piece measures 10 (10,
10½, 10½) inches (25, 25, 27, 27 cm) from the beg,
ending with the RS facing. Adjust the length here, if
you like.

SHAPING THE ARMHOLE

3 BO 5 (5, 6, 6) sts at the beg of the next 2 rows (44,
48, 50, 54) sts.

4 Next row: (RS facing) k1, ssk, knit to last 3 sts,
k2tog, k1.
Next row: k1, purl to last st, k1. Repeat these 2 rows until
36 (38, 40, 44) sts rem.

5 Work straight in St st, remembering to knit the
first and last st of every row, until the work
measures 15 (15½, 16, 16½) inches (38, 39, 41, 42 cm)
from the beg, ending with the WS facing.

SHAPING BACK NECK AND SHOULDERS

6 K1, p6 (6, 7, 8), k22 (24, 24, 26,) p6 (6, 7, 8), k1.
Next row: k8 (8, 9, 10), place these sts on a holder,
BO the center 20 (22, 22, 24) sts, k8 (8, 9, 10).
Continue working the shoulder on these 8 (8, 9, 10) sts,
knitting the first and last st of each row, until the piece
measures 17 (18, 19, 20) inches (43, 46, 48, 51 cm) from
the cast-on edge. Leave the sts on a holder, and return to
the unfinished shoulder sts. Work to match the first
shoulder, leaving the sts on a holder when they're completed.

MAKING THE FRONT

7 Work as given for the back until the work measures 14 (14½, 15, 15½) inches (36, 37, 38, 39 cm)
from the beg.

SHAPING FRONT NECK AND SHOULDERS

8 Work as given for the back until the piece matches
the back in length from the cast-on edge. (To
ensure accuracy, count the number of rows rather than
relying on measuring.) Leave the shoulder sts on
holders as before.

FINISHING THE TOP

9 Place the shoulder sts back on the N's and, with RS
together, work the 3-needle BO. (You may, of
course, BO all the shoulder sts and then seam each
shoulder together, but the 3-needle BO makes a much
neater seam.)

10 Sew up the side seams, and darn in any yarn
ends.

11 Block the top lightly by spraying with water,
and pat to shape. Work one round in sc, if
necessary (see the Summer Shell, page 63).

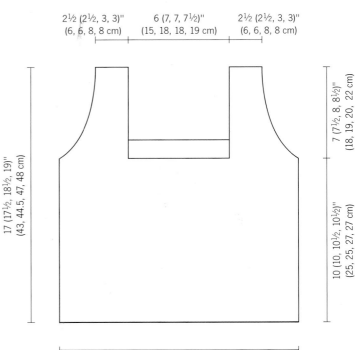

2½ (2½, 3, 3)" (6, 6, 8, 8 cm)   6 (7, 7, 7½)" (15, 18, 18, 19 cm)   2½ (2½, 3, 3)" (6, 6, 8, 8 cm)

7 (7½, 8, 8½)" (18, 19, 20, 22 cm)

17 (17½, 18½, 19)" (43, 44.5, 47, 48 cm)

10 (10, 10½, 10½)" (25, 25, 27, 27 cm)

17 (18, 19, 20)" (43, 46, 48, 51 cm)

Mittens

The cuffs of these mittens give you an opportunity to use a novelty yarn for an eye-catching statement on a simple pair of mittens. The hand of the mitten is knitted in a basic worsted-weight yarn. You get to do your own thing on the cuff, which is generous enough to fit under a jacket sleeve and keep the chill out. And it's such a tiny piece of knitting, you can be as bold as you like with your yarn choice! Use the same yarn on a matching hat (see page 43) to make an attractive set. Keep an eye out for a stunning novelty yarn, and knit up a storm.

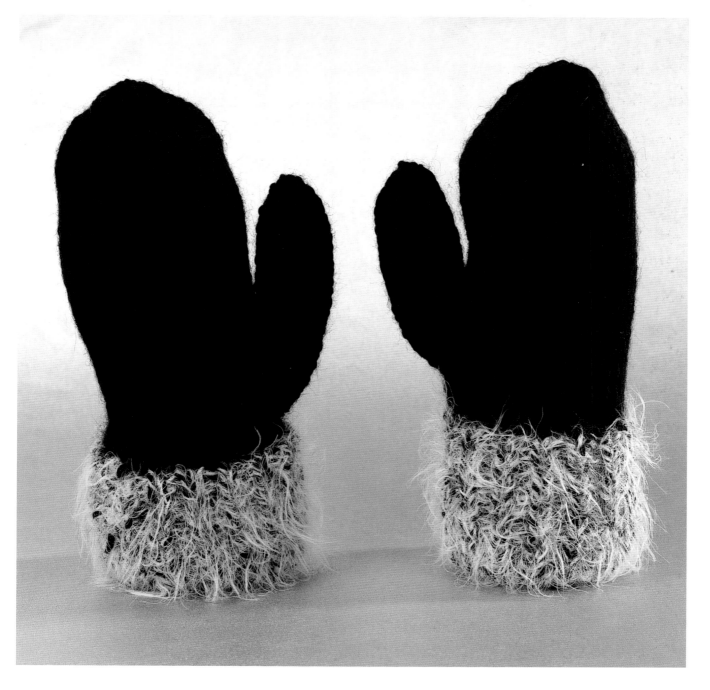

NOTE ON BERROCO'S FURZ: You are by no means limited to this novelty yarn. It's not at all difficult to substitute a yarn of your choice for the cuff, even one of a different weight. The cuff is worked in ribbing, which is by its nature elastic. Check the ball band of your yarn to get an idea what needle size you're likely to need if you're using a much heavier yarn. You might have to adjust the number of stitches for the cuff; if the yarn is a lot thicker, cast on slightly fewer stitches. When the cuff is the required length, increase to the right number of stitches for the hand. If you're really unsure about the size of your cuff, thread a tapestry needle with a smooth yarn and thread it through the cuff stitches. Take them off the knitting needle, and try the cuff around your wrist to decide if you need to add or subtract stitches.

SPECIAL NOTE ON NEEDLE SIZES: As you will be knitting the cuff in a novelty yarn, it's quite possible that you'll use a larger size needle for the cuff than for the hand of the mitten.

MAKING THE RIGHT-HAND MITTEN

1 Work the cuff. Using Furz and size 8 needles, CO 36 sts and work 3 inches (8 cm) in k1p1 rib. (If you want to fold back the cuff, knit for 6 inches [15 cm] or to your desired length of the cuff.) Cut the yarn.

Next row: Change to size 7 N's and the main yarn. Work in St st, beg with a knit row, and inc 4 sts evenly across the row (40 sts). Work 3 more rows, ending with the RS facing.

2 Work the thumb gusset.
Row 1: k22, inc, k2, inc, k16 (42 sts).
Row 2 and every alt row: purl.
Row 3: k22, inc, k4, inc, k16 (44 sts).
Row 5: k22, inc, k6, inc, k16 (46 sts).
Row 7: k22, inc, k8, inc, k16 (48 sts).
Row 9: k22, inc, k10, inc, k16 (50 sts).
Row 11: k22, inc, k12, inc, k16 (52 sts).
Row 13: k22, inc, k14, inc, k16 (54 sts).
Row 14: purl.

3 Divide the sts for the thumb: k22 sts, and slip them onto a stitch holder; k16, and place the rem 16 sts on another holder. Work until the thumb is 2 inches (5 cm) long, ending with the RS facing. (At this point, I like to place the thumb stitches on a safety pin, so I can adjust the length once the hand is complete and the mitten can be tried on. If you feel yours is the right length, then go ahead and complete the thumb here. Otherwise, slip the 16 sts onto a safety pin and cut the yarn, leaving a tail of yarn to use later.)

5 Work the hand. With the RS facing, replace the two sets of sts on holders onto the N's, rejoin the yarn to the unworked sts on the left needle, and knit to the end of the row (38 sts).

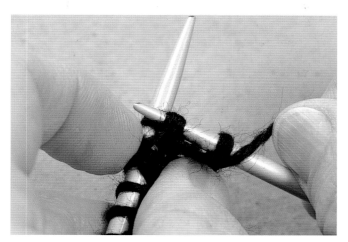

4 Complete the thumb. Next row, k2tog to end of row (8 sts). Purl the next row, then k2tog to the end. Cut the yarn, thread a tapestry needle, and draw through the rem 4 sts. Pull the sts up tightly and fasten off.

6 Work in St st until the mitten is long enough to reach to the tip of the little finger, ending with the RS facing. Begin shaping the top of the hand.

Row 1: k1, ssk, k14, k2tog, ssk, k14, k2tog, k1 (34 sts).
Row 2: purl.
Row 3: k1, ssk, k12, k2tog, ssk, k12, k2tog, k1 (30 sts).
Row 4: purl.
Row 5: k1, ssk, k10, k2tog, ssk, k10, k2tog, k1 (26 sts).
Row 6: p1, p2tog, p8, p2tog tbl, p2tog, p8, p2tog tbl, p1 (22 sts).
Row 7: k1, ssk, k6, k2tog, ssk, k6, k2tog, k1 (18 sts).
Row 8: p1, p2tog, p4, p2tog tbl, p2tog, p4, p2tog tbl, p1 (14 sts).
Row 9: k1, ssk, k2, k2tog, ssk, k2, k2tog, k1 (10 sts).
Arrange the sts on the N's for the 3-needle BO, RS together, and BO the sts using a 3rd needle.

MAKING THE LEFT-HAND MITTEN

7 Work as given for the right mitten to the start of the thumb gusset. Next row, RS facing: k16, inc, k2, inc, k22. Complete in the same way as the right mitten.

FINISHING THE MITTENS

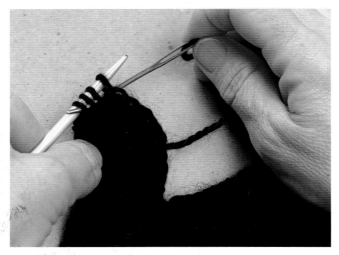

8 For each, sew up the side seam of the mitten. If you left the thumb sts on a holder, try the mitten on to adjust the length of the thumb, then complete it. Sew up the thumb seam. Darn in any loose ends. Block the mittens lightly.

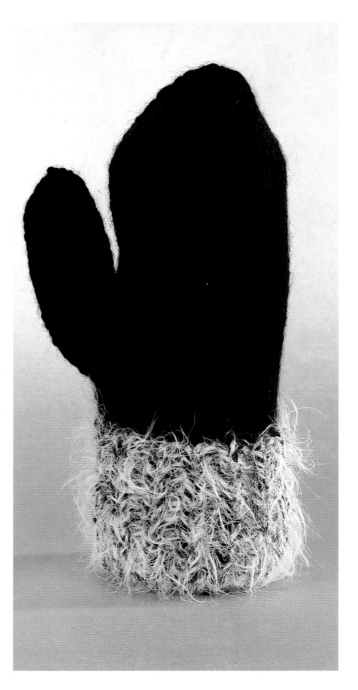

Evening (or Anytime) Wrap

This lovely wrap takes only a few hours to knit in a very simple but striking stitch. If you prefer, you may follow the bonus instructions included here to make this as a scarf. Whether you knit the wrap, the scarf, or both, you'll be sure to find these pieces very useful.

7 balls of Trendsetter Yarn's "Dune," 1¾ oz (50 g) = 90 yds (81 m)

Knitting needles in size 11 US (8 mm), or size necessary to achieve correct gauge

GAUGE

9 sts = 4 inches (10 cm), measured over St st

NOTE: The lacy nature of the pattern and the fluid drape of the wrap mean that the gauge achieved will vary, depending on the knitter and the yarn. This is a project where gauge is obviously not crucial to the fit, so there's no need to fuss too much—hooray!

FINISHED MEASUREMENTS

Approximately 72 x 22 inches (183 x 56 cm)

PATTERN STITCH

Rows 1-6: p1 (yrn, p2tog) to last st, p1.

Rows 7-12: knit (3 g st ridges).

SOME NOTES BEFORE YOU BEGIN

• Work on a test swatch until you're comfortable with the lace pattern.
• When joining in a new ball of yarn, do so on the g st areas, as it's much easier to darn in the ends here.

MAKING THE WRAP

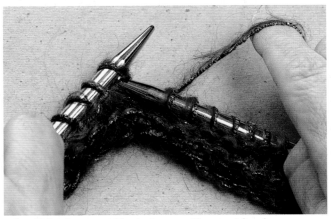

1 CO 50 sts, and knit 6 rows (3 g st ridges).

2 Work the 12-row pattern stitch for the required length, ending with a 12th row.

3 BO *loosely*.

FINISHING

4 Darn in the yarn ends, and snuggle into the softness!

BONUS

You can easily adapt this design to make a scarf. CO 22 sts, and work as given for the desired length. A scarf measuring about 10 x 60 inches (25 x 152 cm) will require approximately 3 balls of yarn.

Strappy Little Bag

Creating your own yarn is part of the fun of this project. Pay a visit to a yarn store, or search through your stash for those forgotten treasures—you don't need very much. You may find a yarn that's ideal just as it is, but by combining a highly textured novelty yarn with a second yarn to give it more body, you can achieve a stunning effect that's all yours. It's important to choose yarns that will knit up into a fairly firm fabric, so those with a high cotton content work very well. And don't ignore the yarns and threads you can find in the embroidery department, as many of these are suitable.

Yarns of choice (As each bag will be unique, I can give you only a rough guide on amount, but in general, a bag of this size uses little yarn. I made the one shown here with two different yarns: a variegated cotton and a novelty mix of synthetic yarns. I needed less than 1¾ oz [50 g].)

Beads, if desired

Embroidery floss in a coordinating color

Knitting needles of an appropriate size

Crochet hook, (if you're using one), or purchased cord

GAUGE

For the bag shown here, 4 sts = 1 inch (2.5 cm), using needles in size 8 US (5 mm), but the gauge will vary considerably depending on the yarns you use. What is important is that you knit to a firm gauge, quite a bit tighter than you would use for a garment. Make at least two test swatches before you begin, to ensure that you like the way the fabric feels and that you're comfortable with the needle size. Then, measure your swatch to establish the number of stitches that you're getting to the inch (cm). Multiply this number by six, and the result is the number of stitches you will need to cast on.

FINISHED MEASUREMENTS

The bag shown measures 6 x 6 inches (15 x 15 cm). Since it's an evening bag, you probably won't want to make yours much larger.

MAKING THE BAG

1 CO the required number of sts (I needed 25), and knit 4 rows. These will give you 2 ridges of g st. Continue in St st, knitting the first and last st of each row, so you have a nice edge, until the work measures about 13 inches (33 cm) from the cast-on edge. End with a purl row.

2 Knit 4 rows (2 g st ridges)
BO all sts.

MAKING THE CORD

3 For my bag, I used 4 ends of yarn and crocheted a chain of 36 inches (91 cm), using a large size crochet hook. This makes a more substantial cord, but you can make yours as thick or as thin as you like. You may also be able to find a suitable, ready-made cord at a fabric store; look in the drapery department.

FINISHING THE BAG

4 Choose which will be the right side of the fabric you've created, and fold your rectangle so that the bag measures approx 6 inches (15 cm) in length, with a 3-inch (8 cm) flap. If necessary, press your bag into shape with a damp cloth and a warm iron, but check the ball bands of the yarn(s) you've used for specific ironing instructions. You don't want your lovely bag-to-be to suffer a meltdown. If you feel heat is not the best method for shaping your bag, spray your folded bag lightly with water, and press the edges down firmly by hand. Leave it to dry.

5 Sew the side seams firmly together with a strong yarn or thread. I oversewed mine on the right side, taking a st between each g st ridge, using a matching embroidery floss. This floss comes in an enormous color range, and you can easily separate the strands, making it very useful when you're knitting with a yarn that's difficult to work with for seaming. The sts disappear very nicely into the fabric while sewing like this from the right side, resulting in a less-bulky seam. You may, of course, seam your bag any way you like.

7 The flap on this bag is embellished with beads purely for decorative purposes; it stays in place without help. If you like, you may sew snaps in place to secure the flap, or use a button and loop.

Wasn't that great fun! Now I ask you, can you really only make one?

6 Sew the cord firmly in place just under the flap. If you like, thread the cord through beads first, as I did, for a really nice touch. (You'll probably need to go to a specialty bead store to find something suitable.)

ACKNOWLEDGMENTS

Considerable thanks are due to my publisher, Carol Taylor, for the opportunity to write this book, and my long-suffering editor, Paige Gilchrist, who worked tirelessly. Many thanks to Sally Poole, who helped with the knitting and in several other ways; Jane Lippmann, for her loyal support; and Dawn Cusick, who has become a dear friend. Suzanne Middlebrooks, owner of Hill Country Weavers in Austin, cheerfully located yarns and ordered them for me. My heartfelt thanks to the wonderful team at Lark, particularly the ever-patient Evan Bracken, for his excellent photography; and my art director, Celia Naranjo, for her enthusiasm and expertise. And last, but most importantly, my husband Ron, without whom this book would not have been possible.

ABOUT THE AUTHOR

Born in Scotland, Catherine Ham grew up in South Africa, where she knitted her first sweater for a Brownie badge. Her lifelong passion for textiles has resulted in a large collection, particularly of ethnic and antique knitting, as well as needlework tools. She and her husband divide their time between their homes in Texas and Europe. She keeps both well stocked with knitting yarns. Cathy's first book is the successful 25 Gorgeous Sweaters for the Brand-New Knitter *(Lark Books, 2000).*

BIBLIOGRAPHY

Buss, Katharina. *Big Book of Knitting*. New York City, New York: Sterling Publishing, 1996.

Newton, Deborah. *Designing Knitwear*. Newtown, Connecticut: Taunton Press,1992.

Stanley, Montse. *Knitter's Handbook*. Pleasantville, New York: Reader's Digest, 1999.

Vogue Knitting, eds. Vogue Knitting: *The Ultimate Knitting Book*.
New York City, New York: Sixth & Spring Publishing, 2002.

Zimmerman, Elizabeth. *Knitting Without Tears*. New York City,
New York: Simon and Schuster, 1973

A NOTE ABOUT SUPPLIERS

Usually, the supplies you need for making the projects in Lark books can be found at your local craft supply store, discount mart, home improvement center, or retail shop relevant to the topic of the book. Occasionally, however, you may need to buy materials or tools from specialty suppliers. In order to provide you with the most up-to-date information, we have created a list of suppliers on our website, which we update on a regular basis. Visit us at www.larkbooks.com, click on "Craft Supply Sources," and then click on the relevant topic. You will find numerous companies listed with their web address and/or mailing address and phone number.

INDEX